Publications of the

MINNESOTA HISTORICAL SOCIETY

RUSSELL W. FRIDLEY

Editor and Director

JUNE DRENNING HOLMQUIST

Managing Editor

The Saga of Saga Hill

THE
SAGA
OF
SAGA
HILL

by Theodore C. _Christian_ Blegen

❧❧❧

MINNESOTA HISTORICAL SOCIETY
St. Paul   1971

CONTENTS

LAKE MINNETONKA

WAYZATA •

SAGA HILL

MARKVILLE •

WEST ARM

MOUND •

SPRING PARK

EXCELSIOR

MINNEAPOLIS | ST. PAUL

LAKE MINNETONKA

A WORD OF EXPLANATION

THIS STORY did not get started in a mood of nostalgia, though it harks back to childhood scenes and experiences more than a half century ago. What set it off was not a spark of emotion about the "good old days," but the reading, a few years ago, of a book of ancient letters translated from the Latin. They happened to be the letters of Pliny the Younger, who saw the volcanic eruption that buried the city of Pompeii and who was a good friend of the Emperor Trajan. But the letters that caught my interest were not those telling about spectacular events or famous people. They were the ones describing Pliny's summer place, his "Laurentine Villa," and its many attractions.

These letters somehow made life in the Roman Empire about a century after Christ seem real and vivid, and the explanation, I thought, lay in the simple and very human detail that Pliny gave about his vacation villa. He told about his gardens planted with fig and mulberry, rosemary, box, and vine. He mentioned his baths and swimming pool, the tennis court, the garden house, and the fishing of soles and prawns. And he also touched upon the charm of visiting friends who came out from Rome to spend a few days with him.

This Roman gentleman of more than eighteen centuries ago seemed almost like a neighbor at Saga Hill on Lake Minnetonka. As I reread his letters I began to wonder if it might not be worthwhile to record the experiences of a family of modern times that found satisfactions and rewards, not in the delights of a Laurentine villa, but in spending its summers, year after year, by the waters of Minnetonka, not far from Minneapolis.

When I began to consider the story, my thoughts were centered on Minnetonka, the lake, and its summer saga, but as it grew, I found it focusing more and more on a chronicle or portait of a family — and especially the life of its children — in the 1890's and 1900's. Minnetonka is a beautiful lake, but lakes are many; the social institution known as the summer vacation is very general; but the family is universal. So this story became a family story.

It was a lucky circumstance for me that father, late in his life, wrote his reminiscences and included a chapter on his summer home. That chapter helped me to get at the beginnings of Saga Hill and also gave me father's own reflections on the interest and value of our summer experiences. And it was no less lucky for me that four critical brothers and sisters read my successive drafts, helped me to fill them out with episodes that I had forgotten, and corrected me with family frankness when my own memory played tricks on me.

T.C.B.

I

THE SAGA BEGINS

THIS is the saga of Saga Hill, a summer colony established in the 1880's on the north shore of West Arm in Lake Minnetonka, not far from Spring Park, and only some twenty-five miles from Minneapolis.

I can not tell the story in full, but I can give some glimpses of it from the point of view of one family. Father, one of the early members of the colony, has left a faithful record of Saga Hill in a volume of reminiscences that he wrote for his children. Starting in 1891, I spent my own summers at Saga Hill for many years. I got out to Minnetonka, I may add, about as soon as humanly possible, for I was born that summer of 1891 in Minneapolis and, according to reliable family tradition, started for the lake about two weeks later. And if our life at the lake does not seem to have left many contemporary records, such as letters and diaries, it is still vivid in the memories of my brothers and sisters and myself.

Our memories and the narrative of father differ just a little. He does not, for example, mention the annual visits of the gypsies, with whom we traded pickerel and dogfish for toys and trinkets — a fairly sharp bargain on our part, for mother in any case would not have cooked the dogfish. She liked neither dogfish nor bullheads, chiefly, I think, because they were ugly.

Nor does father touch on our hunts through the woods for ginseng, from which we expected to reap a fortune, digging up the plants wherever we found them and transplanting them to a shaded part of our yard. We anticipated crops that ultimately would be shipped to China, where, we were told, people found — or believed they found — healing qualities in the grotesque, man-shaped roots. We watched and cared for our ginseng garden and dreamed of great profits, but the fortune, somehow, remained in far-off China. Ultimately, alas, our dreams were shattered by a ginseng thief who raided our precious garden during our absence in town.

Another memory is that of the annual excursion of the family on the glamorous "City of Saint Louis." This was an all-day affair that began when we rowed across West Arm to Spring Park. There we took a morning train for Wayzata, where we embarked upon the great steamer of the lake, usually with the Wilhelm Pettersen family, friends and neighbors from Minneapolis. The "City of Saint Louis," with its three decks, had a capacity of a thousand passengers. Randolph Edgar tells us that it was launched in 1881 and was "the first inland vessel of the United States to be lighted by electricity and was generally considered the finest product of boat building in western waters." On the great sidewheeler, which had a length of a hundred and sixty feet, we saw that captain of Minnetonka captains, John R. Johnson, and we knew a touch of envy of father, a teacher of Greek, who chatted with the captain as if he were the captain's equal. To us the captain was a monarch — like the pilot in Mark Twain's stories of the Mississippi.

Vividly remembered, too, are the hoarse whistle of the red-painted passenger steamer of West Arm, the "Florence M. Deering," and the sight of its bewhiskered captain, Charles W. Deering. Now and then he would let us make the rounds of West Arm with him, and once, after taking a drink from a flask kept in a convenient spot, he delivered himself of a bit of philosophic if grimly retrospective wisdom in the following line: "What I want" — and at that point he took another drink and wiped his long whiskers — "is peace in the family!" Whether or not he had peace in the family, I do not know, though I am under the impression that his marital life perhaps was not without certain storms. He lived on an island across West Arm from Saga Hill, to us a somewhat mysterious place that we rarely visited. On dark summer nights we could see lights blinking from his house, which was partially hidden by the heavy foliage of the island. On fishing trips to Harrison's Bay or shopping trips to Cook's Bay and Mound, we passed by the island; occasionally we landed there to catch frogs; but we kept a wary eye out for the old captain, of whom we were a little afraid though he really was a kindly old man. Sometimes we and our neighbors chartered the "Florence M. Deering" for a long day's trip. The captain would carry passengers to catch the morning train for town, then return to our dock, and we would scramble into the steamboat with our picnic baskets. Then we made the rounds of arms and bays and channels, going as far as Excelsior, before we started homeward in time for the captain to meet the evening train from Minneapolis. Such trips gave us an idea of the size and variety of the lake as a whole, with its bays, channels, islands, and points. Seeing it in 1852, Governor Alexander Ramsey made use of two Sioux names — *mini* (water) and *tonka* (big) — and coined the name "Minnetonka." "Big water" it was to him — and to us.

To these items, all omitted in father's recollections, add the hunting of black raspberries in wild spots long since tamed, including the wilderness of Phelps Island, now crowded with cabins; many fishing trips to Harrison's Bay

when that bay seemed to be full of large pickerel; schooling
in the art of fishing from a father who had a Waltonian
instinct for finding the favorite spots of the lurking pickerel; and a boy's impressions of a Great Northern train
conductor, Mr. Woolnough, whose voice singing out
"Orono" and "Wayzata" and "Minneapolis" still sounds
in my memory. His position as the uniformed commander
of the train seemed the answer to all earthly ambitions.
Add also the glamor of the Minnetonka steamboats, especially the "Belle of Minnetonka," the great rival of the
"City of Saint Louis," and many others, including the
"Hattie May," the "Hebe" (which figures in Oliver Optic's
story of "The Young Hermit"), the "Saucy Kate," the
"Victor," the "Puritan," the "Pilgrim," the "John Alden,"
and the "Ypsilanti."

And add the charm of ferns and flowers, including the
moccasin and lotus, white and yellow lilies, and many
others that mother joined us in collecting on long rowing
trips to Jenning's or Halstead's Bay, where we went with
loaded picnic baskets; the mystery of unexplored woods,
and the summer-long symphony of insects and frogs in the
marshes and along the lake shore, to whose chants and
rhythmic croaking one went to sleep in the three-tier bunks
of our sleeping room.

One recalls, too, the impact of the many odd personalities that had a way of turning up at our summer home,
including a witty and swift-spoken Dane named Hoffmann,
a gardener who had fought in the Dano-Prussian War, had
a liking for children, and delighted us with his stories and
anecdotes. He was a bearded giant who spoke with clipped
accents in a Danish brogue, liked jokes, and had a passion
for flowers. At his place, near Jenning's Bay, he cultivated
a fabulous garden of his own. My sister Anne once visited

his garden with a group of her friends and asked him for the names of three species of flowers that she could not identify. "This one," he said, looking at her, "is known as 'Anne.' " Then glancing at two of the Nydahl girls, he added, "And these two are called 'Agnes' and 'Ragna.' "

Other memories include an extensive business with the Hotel Del Otero at Spring Park that netted in a day as much as sixty cents for twelve dozen frogs caught in the marshes and meadows adjoining the lake and along the shores — money that proved handy in buying firecrackers for the Fourth of July. And of course there were daily excursions to the traditional swimming hole, where a great tree, extending almost straight out over the water, furnished at once a diving board and branches in which to ruminate on the wonders of life.

The Saga Hill story was not one of play and diversion alone. There was much work to do, and father, who had a philosophy of work, daily assigned jobs to his sons, from spring to autumn, which had to be done before play could begin, or interrupted games in progress. His favorite morning greeting to us was, "Boys, this is a working day!" The problem of the day's work led to a game of wits between two generations, father on the one side, his sons on the other. We thought we had triumphed when at last we persuaded him, instead of having us work at odd times throughout the day, to give us a particular job or set of jobs for a given day. He wracked his brains to think up work for us, and with this concession we nearly broke up the summer home by getting up very early in the morning and completing the entire task soon after breakfast time, leaving the normal day open for important enterprises, such as fishing, swimming, and games. But father was not easy to outwit. He complimented us on our energy and

increased the size of the jobs assigned to us. Ultimately he
ran out of big jobs, and we were obliged to return to the
system of work assignments whenever he found it expedient
to make them — a system we detested, for often it broke
off a game of shinny or "can-can" at a crucial moment.
I have been interested to find that in his recollections he
writes about his plan of having his sons do regular work
during the mornings of vacation days. He says that after
he had assigned the daily job, his boys rushed at it as if
their very lives were at stake — and he believes that if they
later demonstrated a will to work, the Minnetonka experience possibly had a little influence on their attitude. The
girls were not left out of the picture, for they too had their
tasks to do, usually in the house, but sometimes with the
boys in the gardens.

Our experiences probably were more or less typical of
life during Minnetonka summers at all parts of the lake—
and indeed at thousands of other American lakes not
blessed with the name "Minnetonka." If there was something unusual about Saga Hill summer life, it is to be
explained by the nature of the colony itself, the interests
of its members, and the circumstance that it formed a fairly
homogeneous and well-knit society.

In his reminiscences, father tells of the beginnings of
the colony. A group of professors, ministers, bankers, and
professional men, most of them members of the Trinity
Lutheran Church in Minneapolis and deeply interested in
the affairs of Augsburg Seminary and College, where father
taught, formed, in June 1885, the "Saga Hill Association."
With a capital stock of ten thousand dollars, they pur-
chased from a farmer a forty-acre tract of land lying in the
area nearly surrounded by West Arm, North Arm, and
Forest Lake, divided this land into lots, and arranged for

each member to have a sizable frontage on West Arm, with lots reaching far back into the woods. Father bought five shares in the association in the spring of 1886, and, as we later believed, picked or was allotted some of the best lakeshore property on West Arm.

It may be of interest to mention some of the personalities in the Saga Hill Association. Its president was a banker, Reinert Sunde, and its secretary was M. Falk Gjertsen, a very eloquent, popular, and highly controversial Norwegian-American preacher who wrote a Norwegian-American novel in his later years. Another member was Olaf Hoff, an engineer of Old World education and wide interests. He was notable as a bridge builder who later won fame for constructing, first, the Detroit River Tunnel—he was then vice-president of the Butler Brothers - Hoff Company —and later the tunnel under the Harlem River in New York. Yet another colony member was Sven Oftedal, professor at Augsburg College and later its president, an orator and scholar feared for his wit and admired for his versatility, a student of many languages, including Greek, ancient and modern, and one of the builders of the Minneapolis Public Library system. Our own immediate neighbors for a time in the earlier years, antedating my memory, were the Uelands of Minneapolis. Judge Andreas Ueland was a well-known figure in the city, noted for the wit and irony of his after-dinner speeches, and Mrs. Ueland was a civic leader and feminist for whom mother had great admiration.

Among others associated with the colony were Odin Moe, a Minneapolis businessman, and Lars Swenson, a veteran of the Civil War, the manager of the Augsburg Publishing House, and in the late 1880's a state senator. It was Swenson who sold half of his shares in the association to father (for $750) and thus made it possible for our family to be a part of the Saga Hill colony.

Some years later, as the colony expanded to the shores of the near-by Forest Lake, Georg Sverdrup, president of Augsburg and in my father's opinion the foremost theological thinker and scholar among the Norwegian Americans, joined the settlement, along with several other Augsburg professors. Sverdrup, after renting a cottage for a summer or two, bought land on Forest Lake, including a couple of lots from father, and later built a summer home of his own in which he planned to live the year round after his retirement. Among other Augsburg professors attracted to the shores of Forest Lake was H. N. Hendrickson, a classicist, historian, and singer under whom, when my brothers and I were students at Augsburg, we all studied Latin. He also directed a college sextet of which I was a member, and for two summers (1909 and 1912) we made extensive tours throughout the Middle West giving concerts. Yet another professor was H. A. Urseth, a poet and teacher of English, a man of sensitive mind and wide reading with whom my brothers and I studied writing and English literature. He also had deep musical interests and at Augsburg directed the band, which I succeeded in joining after a summer of cheek-bursting practice on the cornet. As two of my brothers played the clarinet, it will be understood that the vicinity of the Blegen house was probably not too soothing an environment for tired professorial nerves. Another teacher in the group was J. L. Nydahl, a man of Christian integrity and gentleness. N. N. Ronning, the magazine editor, writer, and humorist, was also a member of the Forest Lake settlement for a few years, and some years later it was joined by Professor Andreas Helland, a theologian of learning and wit who edited the extensive writings of

Sverdrup and in the 1940's published an excellent biography of him. All these men were valued colleagues and friends of my father. Their presence and that of their families added much to the interest and character of the summer colony.

Father had his house built by 1887, and that was therefore his first summer at West Arm. It was a two-story house, with a tower at one corner that served as a sanctuary for bats, long porches, a summer kitchen some distance behind the house, a windmill with pipes running down to the lake, a shower house, and a coffee house that ultimately was completely covered, top and sides, by wild grape vines. The first two summers were busy ones, for much of the building was carried on in that period. A well was dug the first summer, then deepened and equipped with cement walls and pump the second. Father went to St. Paul to buy a boat. He gave a painter one of his wood lots in return for painting the exterior of the house, and he himself decorated the interior. He embarked upon a planting program that included a row of cedar trees, some of which, venerable and wide-spreading, still stand along the West Arm shore and doubtless still invite, as they did years ago, the annual return of cedar birds. Father also planted apple trees, grapes, raspberries, and many kinds of vegetables.

Mother, a lover of flowers, gave much attention, as the years went by, to a flower garden of symmetrical pattern, with graveled paths and many beds. Here she had flowers all summer long — roses (white, pink, red, and yellow), peonies, snowballs, hydrangeas, verbena, four o'clocks, bachelor's buttons, moss roses, sweet alyssum, mignonette, pinks, pansies, nasturtiums, sweet peas, iris, tiger lilies, and of course lilacs. Flowers both in the garden and from the woods were always a part of the summer life.

A near-by farmer delivered milk daily. Groceries were at first brought from Markville, now Crystal Bay, a long distance in that pre-automobile day, and the lake supplied fish, not indeed the soles and prawns of which Pliny spoke, but sunfish, crappies, black bass, and pickerel (northern pike), the latter often running to eight or ten pounds and beyond (and sometimes running beyond our ability to land them).

Meanwhile, the Saga Hill Association had built, not far from our place, a clubhouse, or more correctly, a meeting-house, near the lake shore. There, on Sundays, regular services were held, with Sunday school for the children, of whom, in the various families, there were many, father's family contributing — over a stretch of fourteen years — four boys and two girls to the younger society.

Father devotes some attention in his recollections to the affairs of the meetinghouse, which came to a sad end. In the late 1880's and early 1890's the Norwegian Lutherans, after a period of theological warfare marked by everything but shooting, were engaged in an effort to unite four synods or church groups, and they did in fact create what was called the United Norwegian Lutheran Church of America. Unhappily, however, this movement toward union got involved in difficulties with respect to the control of Augsburg College and Seminary, and the upshot of it was that the friends of that institution created a synod of their own, the Lutheran Free Church. This controversy resulted in the closing of the Saga Hill meetinghouse, since some of the members belonged to one group and some to another. The fires of controversy scorched the summer church. So it was sold and moved away, to the genuine regret of members of the younger generation who had made its floors and roof the playground for certain running, hiding, and leaping games that were somewhat outside the plans of the colony founders.

The Free Church people, however, bought the home of A. C. Haugan, one of the Saga Hill members, by an arrangement worked out by my father and Gjertsen, and created from it a large summer house for the nurses in the Deaconess Hospital of Minneapolis. For many years thereafter every summer Sunday morning saw the colony, insofar as its church affiliations did not prove an obstacle, meet for sermons and church singing on the wide verandas of the Deaconess Home. There father, Oftedal, Sverdrup, Hendrickson, Nydahl, Helland, and other Augsburg professors, and many visiting ministers, took turns in preaching sermons that were punctuated by the throaty whistle of Captain Deering's steamboat, with every youngster squirming in his seat to get a look at the passing vessel and perhaps, for a brief moment, to escape the impact of Lutheran theology.

This was the setting of the Minnetonka life that went on, summer after summer, in the 1890's and the 1900's, sometimes in the absence of father. He devoted the summer of 1898 to a European trip, on which he took with him my brother Hal; twelve years later he went to Scotland and Norway (with Carl); and he often was away on speaking trips or engaged in committee activities that made it impossible for him to devote full time to the lake, whose life he and mother loved.

II

◇◇

VISITORS AND HOUSEHOLD PROBLEMS

ONE of the interesting, if to mother burdensome, aspects of Saga Hill life was the unending stream of visitors who came, often without warning, to stay a day or a few days or a few weeks, if not the entire summer. Our recollection of the summers at Minnetonka, before we sold our large West Arm place, is of visitors all summer long. Father writes much about some of them, notably President Sverdrup, who later, as I have said, built a cottage of his own only a short distance from our place. He describes Sverdrup as follows: "He was a pleasant person to have as a guest, neat and orderly in bearing, rich in knowledge and interesting in conversation, a man one could respect." He records the contrast and clash of personalities between Sverdrup and the famed Norwegian missionary-scholar, Lars O. Skrefsrud. The latter, a linguist, orator, and hunter, seemed to us to be a kind of potentate, an imperious master of men who, for all we knew, was a maharaja in distant India, from which he came — and indeed he was something like that. Upon his first visit, a meeting was held for him in the Spring Park pavilion, where he spoke to a big audience, and afterward mother and father gave a dinner for him, with many guests who, father records, continued their lively conversation on into the afternoon.

On another occasion Skrefsrud interrupted a speaking tour to spend a vacation at our home and made a tremendous impression upon the younger generation. He was a fanatical fisherman who, if he went out for sunfish and crappies, was reluctant to come in until he had caught, in that pre-fishing-license era, a hundred, and when he returned, he insisted upon counting them in state, with mother as a spectator. Needless to say, he never cleaned the fish he caught. That job was turned over to the older boys of the family, and after it was completed mother sent them on the rounds of the neighbors, with parcels of dressed fish as gifts. If they felt some resentment about the necessity of his catching and their cleaning a hundred fish, they were careful not to offend him by voicing it. Not long ago in a biography of Skrefsrud published in Norway, I found a picture of him and father fishing at Lake Minnetonka, with a Viking boat in the background (probably from the summer of 1895 — Skrefsrud was in America from 1894 until September 1895).

One evening the missionary and President Sverdrup engaged in a lively discussion of the nature of immortality, with father as a listener. The debate went far into the night and finally had to close, with Skrefsrud on the losing end. As father and Skrefsrud were walking home, the latter suddenly stopped and exclaimed, "Oh, fool that I was! I forgot my best argument!" He wanted to return immediately to resume the fight about immortality, but father gently but firmly suggested that the argument was over and that no good purpose would be served by resuming it. For a full generation father was the American secretary for the great mission in the Santhalistan district of India, of which Skrefsrud, in his day, was the head. Father greatly admired Skrefsrud and in his recollections he says, "We were happy to have him as a guest."

Aunt Augusta, a favorite in the family, likes to recall that the great missionary, then a widower, fell in love with a charming young Minneapolis lady during his American visit and frankly discussed with father the problem of marrying her. Father had grave doubts about the wisdom of the proposed match and argued Skrefsrud out of it.

We always took delight in the visits of Augusta — "Gustie," we called her — for she brought with her the atmosphere of the great world. A lady of rare charm, dressed in the height of fashion, interested in boys and girls, and usually arriving with gifts for each one of us, she completely won our hearts. It was exciting when she arrived from Chicago or St. Paul, and Martha and Anne used to watch admiringly as she unpacked her luggage. After Hal and Carl entered the University, they traveled on one occasion to Chicago, where Aunt Gustie then lived, to see Minnesota and Chicago play football in the days when "Eckie, Eckie Eckersall" was in his glory. Our aunt met them after the game, which Minnesota won by a score of 4 to 2, and then crowned the day for them by escorting them to the ill-fated Iroquois Theater, where they saw the inimitable George Cohan in one of those glamorous shows that closed with the unfurling of the flag. That was an occasion never to be forgotten.

Also popular in the family circle was Aunt Clara — another of mother's sisters — who lived in Wisconsin but occasionally came to the lake on visits and spent two entire summers there with her family. Like "Gustie," she was charming, full of humor, and adored by the younger generation. She had a large family, and the cousins contributed to the hilarity of Saga Hill. Aunt Clara's husband — our Uncle George — was a surveyor and woodsman who knew the life of lumber camps in the Wisconsin and Minnesota forests. I have often regretted that he did not spin Paul Bunyan stories to us in those early days. In later years he informed me that he had heard the Bunyan legends told and retold in the Wisconsin woods in the 1890's. This is the only evidence I have ever come across that Paul Bunyan tales were recounted by lumberjacks in the golden age of lumbering. Uncle George was very popular in our circles.

It was a Herculean task for mother to manage her growing summer household, with its swarm of always hungry children, streams of visitors, and no grocery store within easy reach. Fortunately for a family of academic income, maids were not then the luxury they later became, and mother managed not only to have the help of a maid — we always called her "the girl" — but also to keep each one over a period of some years, so that, depending upon her personal traits and ways, she was likely to seem almost a member of the family. In the earlier years there was the dark-haired Annette, still remembered more than a half century later. She was a strict disciplinarian of the children, somewhat austere and forbidding, but devoted to the family. Naturally we appreciated any episode that threw her dignity a bit off balance. On one occasion she was invited to join the family group that set out by boat in the early evening to get the day's mail at Spring Park. As she started to step off the dock, she perched precariously with one foot in the boat and one on the dock. The boat perversely moved away from the dock, and after an instant or two of agonized stretching, Annette tumbled ingloriously into the lake. She gathered herself up and rushed for the house, with everybody shouting with laughter at her dripping discomfiture.

The summer work began in the spring before we "moved out" in May. Father recalls, incidentally, that the eagerness of the family to get out to Saga Hill in the spring was almost agonizing in its intensity. But we did not just go to the station and board a train for Spring Park. "Moving out" was not quite so simple as that. There were elaborate preparations. First, there was the inevitable purchase of a barrel of *kavrings* (rusks), useful at any and all times to still the pangs of hunger. Large boxes of soda and graham crackers were bought, as well as hundred-pound sacks of flour and sugar, plus hams and various smoked meats. Finally, on a day of excited anticipation, the Minnetonka farmer, Ole Moe, would drive up to our house in town, and our supplies were piled into his lumber wagon, together with boxes loaded with hundreds of empty jars and glasses and sundry trunks, parcels, and bags. The boy — usually Hal, Carl, or John — given the honor of driving out with Ole Moe was envied. He obviously was born under a lucky star. John recalls an occasion when he and father drove to the lake with Moe in the lumber wagon, going by way of Golden Valley. A day or two later, the whole family would start for Minnetonka by train, each member carrying as many bags and parcels as he or she could, everybody excited and happy. At Spring Park father or one of the boys would meet us with the boat, and then, with our nerves tingling, we would row across West Arm to Saga Hill and the adventures of the summer would begin. One time, arriving at Spring Park, I admired the men who cleverly hopped off the train before it stopped. Unhappily I failed to observe their technique, and so I jumped straight out from the train step, and carried one arm in a sling for some weeks as a result of the tumble I took.

At the lake the problem of milk for the children was acute. For some years a farm boy, entrancing to us because he had St. Vitus Dance and stuttered, delivered the milk, always arriving with the milk can in one hand and a quart measuring cup in the other. At a period antedating my memory, father decided that the most effective way of meet-

ing the milk problem was to rent a cow from an obliging
farmer. This he did for several years, pasturing the creature
on Forest Lake grounds that later were transformed into a
summer home by Professor Hendrickson. The "girl" did
the milking, with the boys and Martha using switches to
brush off flies and thus avoid any bovine irritation that
might upset the milk can.

We were a Puritan household in which strong drink
was regarded as the special invention of the Devil. Our
standard drinks were water, milk, coffee, and tea; but
father liked grape juice, lemonade, and root beer. Occasionally, on hot summer days, therefore, we had cooling drinks
of these varieties. Our root beer, of course, was made at
home. Father would concoct a tubful of it and bottle the
liquid for future use. Coca Cola had not yet appeared on
the scene, but on expeditions to Spring Park or to a country
store we usually celebrated by drinking a bottle of fizzing
pop — an extravagance, of course, for it meant the heavy
expenditure of five hard-earned pennies.

All summer long the boardwalk connecting the kitchen
with the summer kitchen was much traveled, and on certain
special occasions the children had a way of clustering
around the door of the summer kitchen. There was no
smell more alluring than that pouring out of that intriguing
structure when cookies, cakes, or doughnuts were being
baked. So we stood about, hoping for a bowl to scrape
with our fingers or for any cookies or crumbs that might
come our way. If we managed to secure a fair supply,
supplemented by such tidbits as we could snare from the
garden or orchard, we were likely to climb a great tree
near the kitchen, in the branches of which we had built
board seats for ourselves, each one individually initialed
and claimed. In this tree house we ate in Olympian peace.

Occasionally we feasted daringly on the little platform at the very top of the windmill.

The characteristic kitchen smell at dinner time was, of course, that of frying fish. All summer long pan fish supplied the main dinner course, and mother was a past master in the art of preparing sunfish, our favorite food. But she knew other varieties of fish preparation, including a pickerel soup and boiled fish. The greatest delicacy of the summer, and a rare one, came when she made fish cakes or fish pudding. This was an art carried to America from Norway, where fish pudding, made from halibut and dressed with shrimp sauce, was of a unique excellence. But the Minnetonka fish cakes and fish puddings, which required innumerable grindings, were of such delicacy, fineness, and goodness, that they still remain in my memory as the best food I have ever tasted. I may add that mother and Annette, in considering the feasibility of a meal of fish cakes or pudding, scorned any northern pike that weighed less than five or six pounds. Consequently, when we caught a big one, we might instantly exclaim: "Fish cakes!"

But our meals were not just a matter of main dishes. There was also the never-ending problem of an adequate bread supply, and this was met by regular bread baking on Wednesdays and Saturdays, ordinarily with not less than ten loaves at each baking. In the earlier years, we never bought bread from the grocer — there was, of course, no available bakery — but we were dependent upon the grocer for many kinds of supplies as the summers wore along. Ultimately we were freed from our dependence upon the Markville (Crystal Bay) grocery, with its deliveries once a week from one Stangeland, the first proprietor, and later from a man named Maxwell. One day, as mother was considering just what to order, the groceryman whose horses were waiting on the county road behind our house said, "Hurry, hurry, Mrs. Blegen, I haven't had my dinner yet!" The time came when "Mauny" Nelson and his father set up a store a mile and a half up in the country, off Jenning's Bay, and then we could meet almost any crisis that came along, for we counted it nothing but pleasure and adventure to walk to this country grocery on mother's errands. There was always the fun, after we entered the store to the tinkling of a bell, of exploring the counter where caramels, many-colored gumdrops, lemon drops, long strings of licorice, and pyramided chocolate-covered candies were displayed, and of buying as many of them as our pennies permitted, with a bottle of strawberry pop included, if we were really flush with money.

Mother faced not only the problem of supplying her family with daily meals (and the food they ate between meals) but also that of laying up a store of canned foods for the long autumn and winter in town. Consequently the kitchens were busy throughout the summer with what seemed to be interminable canning, with Martha — and in later years Anne — joining in the heavy and hot work. This activity normally produced some three hundred or more cans, glasses, and jars of jam, apple butter, jelly, sauces, tomatoes, and pickles each season to be carried back to town and stored away in our fruit cellar. Through all the summer any member of the family who made a trip to Minneapolis—this usually meant father—was loaded down with as heavy a consignment of canned goods as he could possibly carry. All this fitted in with the family philosophy of life at the lake. Minnetonka contributed to the economy of a large family supported by the modest earnings of a teacher in a small denominational college. For one thing, we lived there for a long summer vacation — in the earlier

years father's vacation usually ran from about May 7 to
October 1, and often he and mother maneuvered to get
their children excused from public school before the regular
term ended and, if our marks were not too unpromising, to
have us entered just a little later than the normal opening
of the school year. We also used the summer place to the
economic advantage of the family in meeting the food
problem during the long months of the academic year.
So mother worked hard in the summer to stock the town
cellar. She capitalized on apples, plums, cherries, black
raspberries, and grapes, including wild grapes that we
gathered by tubfuls on family excursions. She did not can
vegetables, except tomatoes, but we carted to town large
quantities of potatoes and buried them in our basement
sand bin. In the late summer we also wrapped apples,
using scraps of newspapers for each one, with the idea that
this would preserve them for winter use. Father grew
many varieties, including Wealthy, Peerless, and Greenings,
and we took as much as we could of our crop to town to
put in our basement or attic.

We were an apple-eating family, and the Minnetonka
apples were supplemented by barrels of "winter apples" —
Winesaps, Baldwins, or Jonathans — bought by father in
the market. He had an inordinate interest in apples and
knew of many kinds. There was rarely a time when we
could not, by making a convenient expedition to the basement, find a good apple to munch. The apple barrel was a
boon to mother in restraining between-meals raids on the
kitchen.

We sometimes had ice during the hot summer months,
borrowed in the earlier years from the Sundes or bought, in
later times, from the grizzled father of Ellwood Nelson,
who (after Captain Deering's day of glory had passed) ran

the West Arm passenger launch; but we never stored up ice in the wintertime for summer use. One of the curious aspects of our Minnetonka experience is that we knew nothing about the lake during the months of snow and ice. To this day I have never fished through the ice at Minnetonka and have never cut a piece of ice from the frozen lake. We simply did not know the ice-covered Minnetonka. But in the summertime our foods did not spoil. And for a good reason — we had a cellar. We had a cellar in the old home on West Arm, and we had one in the house on Forest Lake in later years. There was always the cellar. It was cool for wooden and crockery pans and jars of milk and other foods. In the house on West Arm there was an outside door leading to it, though not the kind one slid on in the then popular song. We lacked the slide, but we did have the rain barrel, also celebrated in song, and it stood near the cellar door. We "hollered" down the rain barrel — and we also watched with interest the squirming animal life in that repository of rain water.

III

ADVENTURES, GAMES, AND HOBBIES

SPRING Park was fascinating to the boys and girls of our family and neighborhood, and we liked nothing better, especially on a Sunday or holiday, than to cross the lake and stroll around the station and picnic grounds.

On holidays, crowds would gather at the old wooden station to await the coming of a "special" from town, every car crowded with pleasure-seekers. Picnics were of every kind. I remember a Spring Park day of sun and blue sky and placid waters, but to my eyes its appeal lay in the fact that the grounds were crowded with people of black color, strange folk of absorbing interest. With my brother John, I stood on the platform as the morning "special" came around the distant bend, the engine belching smoke, the hoarse whistle sounding. A burly black man looked down the long track and exclaimed, "There she comes — she's comin' rough." We seized upon the phrase, and all that summer, on every possible occasion, we shouted, "There she comes — she's comin' rough!"

It is curious how, summer after summer, phrases out of special occurrences were taken up in our daily usage, sometimes for a few weeks or an entire summer, sometimes for many years. One that served us a long time was "Genuine Shirley." Whenever we wanted to convey the idea of high quality or top value, we said, "Genuine Shirley." The phrase came from a brand of suspenders that bore the trademark "Genuine Shirley." We insisted upon having genuine Shirley suspenders (we did not wear belts). Many years later, when speaking of superlative values and objects a world away from the scenes of our boyhood, occasionally we found ourselves saying "Genuine Shirley." Another much, if frivolously, used phrase — perhaps introduced by Carl — was the admonition to "Have no further worry." If guests were coming and mother needed a stupendous catch of fish, one of us would instantly say, "Have no further worry." This implied, of course, that catching a great string of fish was the merest detail, just a bagatelle. If someone voiced concern about a difficult job or problem, he was at once told to have no further worry. It was nothing at all. So, in time, the phrase became a byword, used with mock seriousness on every occasion, even when it was obvious that we could not have the slightest control over an impending event. We picked up with delight, and used again and again, Captain Deering's doleful phrase, "What I want is peace in the family." Let anyone start a quarrel, and immediately he was reminded of the critical importance of peace in the family. Naturally we repeated, though with an ironical tone, father's vigorous, but to us disheartening, morning salutation, "Boys, this is a working day."

The pavilion on Spring Park Bay, with its bowling alleys and soda counter, its long porch looking out across the bay, and its mounds of candy and peanuts and gum, was to us an isle of enchantment. Out front, near the pavilion, was the long Spring Park dock where the steamboats, in all their grandeur, landed. We seldom got a chance to ride in those boats, but it was thrilling to stand on the dock, with eyes wide and nerves tingling, as they came proudly in. We knew their names, their lines, their whistles. "The Puritan," we would say, or "The Mayflower," or "The Ypsilanti," as we heard their whistles far out on the lake. As they docked, ladies in long dresses, and finely dressed men, swarmed out to join the merrymakers of the park. Out on the grounds, baseball games added to the excitement, and, barefooted, we would edge up to spots where we could see the action. Roundabout were tables and benches, families eating picnic lunches, children playing games, and here and there, on winding paths, lovers walking arm in arm or hand in hand (always to us a most intriguing sight). On one side was the famed Hotel Del Otero, with its glimpses of a world of fashion and wealth and ease, as we thought — a society of finery outside our experience, definitely more elegant than the crowds on the picnic grounds. As we walked slowly past, we liked to look, a little enviously, at the "elegant" men and ladies playing croquet on the parked hotel grounds.

Spring Park was a medley of sounds and sights, noises and smells, trains, jostling crowds, steamboats, excitement, fun, a little bowling now and then — and we were mournful when we had to push out our boat and start the long row home. But the melancholy was usually relieved by a bag of caramels, a sack of peanuts, or a package of crackerjack — and the luscious memory of a pineapple or chocolate ice-cream soda. And so we rowed out on the lake with pleasant memories, trailing a trolling line in the hope of adding a big pickerel to the day's excitement.

Drama and near tragedy, not wholly unmixed with comedy, also made their contributions to memories. Among our neighbors in the early days was the Sunde family, a banker with a brood of children that included (besides Alec, Eddy, Elsie, and Amy) Reynold, a stalwart boy who became the hero of Saga Hill because he owned a rifle. When Reynold acquired his rifle, we flocked around him. He took pride in his possession, and when he shot it off, with ten or fifteen youngsters standing admiringly behind him, each one of them ached for the privilege of pulling the trigger.

One day he gave us a demonstration. We trailed along behind him, our eyes popping with every shot. He would pick his target, call to us to stand back, take aim, and fire. Sometimes he hit the target, and if we had had a children's community government, we should have elected him mayor.

Then the rifle wedged. The cartridge did not slip in easily. Reynold, master of the occasion, knew exactly what to do. He put the end of the barrel on the ground and tried to push in the cartridge. The position was a trifle insecure, and so he rested the end of the gun on one foot and shoved and pounded. Suddenly the cartridge not only went in but went off! There was an explosion, and Reynold shrieked. The shot had sliced off his great toe.

Everybody was excited. The first problem was for one of us to rush off and inform somebody. Nobody dared to do it. Finally, by common consent, it was decided that the youngest member of the crowd should let our parents know what had happened. Reynold had shot himself. He was bleeding. We were terrified. We needed help. I was the youngest, and so I was delegated to run for home as hard as I could.

I dashed off, found mother in her garden and ran up to her, out of breath, excited, scared. Family tradition reports essentially the following exchange of words:

"Whatever is the matter, Theodore?" she asked.

"Reynold!" I said, "Reynold, he shot him!"

My mother nearly fainted.

"Theodore," she said, "Who has been shot? What has happened? Quick, tell me." She called for father, who was reading on the long porch.

Father dropped his book and ran out to the garden.

"What is it? What is wrong?"

Mother said, "Theodore says that Reynold has shot somebody, but he is so excited I can't find out who."

Father shook me. "Who has been shot?" he shouted. "Not Carl? Not Halvard? Not John? Not Martha?" All my brothers and sisters (at that time).

"Reynold, he shot him!" I cried.

"Take us to him," father shouted, and off we dashed, father and mother following me.

And so we came upon the ensemble — the crowd of boys and girls standing around Reynold, Reynold with his shoe off, Reynold with his great toe off.

The episode of the rifle fitted in with the spirit of play. In a neighborhood of many boys and girls, one would expect games to be plentiful. We played tag, "Run, Sheep, Run," prisoner's base, "Pump, Pump, Pull Away," baseball, "can-can," shinny, last-couple-out, leapfrog, races on land and in water, and a variety of indoor games. Cards with their aces, kings, and queens — and their wicked associations with gambling — were forbidden in the family, but as we grew older we discovered ways of using, especially in our town house, the innocent game of "Authors" to play whist and certain other card games that father and mother would have condemned if we had used regular playing cards. We sometimes had a suspicion that father knew in a general way what was going on, but if so, he probably consoled himself with the thought that we could not go very far wrong while we held in our hands placards adorned with pictures of Whittier, Longfellow, Lowell, and other bewhiskered writers whose respectability was beyond question. We also played with a set of "Yellowstone" cards, each one decorated with a scene from the great park in the West.

And, of course, we indulged in betting on every possible occasion, though money was a trifle too precious to risk in this sport.

Carl had a talent not only for solving puzzles but also for inventing them, often intricate ones involving links or circles, and we spent hours trying to work them out, while he sat watching us, occasionally making seemingly helpful, but invariably misleading, suggestions.

The games we played helped to strengthen our muscles and perhaps our wits. Sometimes we played dangerous games, particularly tag on the scaffolding of the high windmill or in trees with perilous leaps from branch to branch or from trees to near-by roofs. Water games were plentiful, too, but more often the real dangers came in long-distance swimming along the shore or across West Arm. We might arrange to have a boat accompany us, but frequently, confident of our skill, we swam without any such safeguard.

We had a few minor superstitions and some faith in remedies that had no sanction from medical science. The oozing milk from milkweed was regarded by us as a good remedy for warts, and we knew exactly where the supply was. When any one of us discovered a wart on finger or hand, we made for the milkweed as quickly as possible. If bad luck happened, such as a black cat cutting across our path, we took proper precautions to avoid trouble. We believed it effective to throw a stone or a bit of dirt over the left shoulder. A piece of black thread tied around a finger also had its uses. Soap, water, and bandages we avoided if possible, but now and then cuts were so deep and bloody that we rushed to the house and the care of a mother whose brood of children compelled her to be both doctor and druggist.

Manufactured toys were not plentiful, but it was easy

enough, with house, woods, garden, and lake at our disposal, to find natural materials for games. When we were very small, we had no manufactured trains with tracks, but we made our own cars from boards, 1 by 4 and cut into blocks 8 inches long. These were, of course, freight cars. The engine was cut with a point at the front. Nails at the ends of each car made it possible to string the train together, and a long cord was put into the snout of the engine. There were no tracks, but we worked out our routes along the floors.

We took care, a few years later, to find good shinny clubs from the woods, always looking for straight stems and for roots that had the right shape of club head. We played both can-can (cricket) and shinny (our version of hockey) on the dirt road behind our house.

We also made toy boats, and Carl capped our inventive efforts by building a three-decker modeled after "The City of Saint Louis." When we were a bit older, he also fashioned a golf course in the long front yard that stretched down to the lake. True enough, we did not have greens and cups, golf clubs, or golf balls, but Carl marked out areas around certain trees and then, using our shinny clubs, we drove square wooden blocks to these spots, carefully counting our strokes. We also bowled, using the windmill platform, croquet balls, and ten pins.

The long porch at the front of our summer house was a fishing boat, the ground around it deep water to our imagination — water teeming with fish. We fitted up poles and lines with bent pins as hooks and dropped them down to the ground. Martha was expected to hook leaves onto the bent pins. Every leaf had a piscatorial value. A white oak leaf was a black bass, a maple leaf was a sunfish, ironwood a crappie, the long ribbon grass from the garden a pickerel, basswood a rockbass, elm a dogfish, and a weed a bullhead. We abused Martha shamefully. She had to do the chores. She had to hunt up leaves, attach them to our lines, give our lines tugs to let us know that the fish were striking, and then we would haul in our catches, comparing, classifying, boasting, and then dropping the lines again, always expecting Martha to do the job down below. Arguments arose as to the size of catches. Pickerel and black bass were, of course, choicer than other varieties, and Martha had a way of making such catches rare. When any one of us drew up white oak or ribbon grass, there was a shout of elation. Meanwhile poor Martha almost never had the fun of porch fishing. She was good and efficient at attaching leaves to our hooks — and after all somebody had to do that job.

Somehow Carl was frequently the manager of any undertaking not directed by father or mother. He had a way of turning any task given him into a game, like Tom Sawyer, making it a privilege for us and neighbor boys to pitch in and work. Mother was one of the first in the Saga Hill neighborhood to install a washing machine. It was operated by hand, and she gave the job of turning the handle to the boys. We were proud of the machine. The family, in our judgment, gained prestige from it. It was something to see and admire.

Carl did not shirk his share of the common tasks, but his role was often that of master of ceremonies, and he gave the accolade of champion to the boy who established the highest record. One of Carl's prize possessions was a brass watch. I remember my oldest brother, Hal, furiously working the machine, sweat pouring down his face, while Carl, serene as director of operations, sat on a stump, holding his watch and observing the performance. Each one of us ached to get at the handle and to break the record. Presently the job was done, and Carl was the spokesman in reporting this happy fact to mother. We had similar experiences when she bought a hand-driven ice-cream freezer.

On fishing expeditions father usually sat in the back seat when we rowed across West Arm on our way to Harrison's Bay for pickerel. Normally he timed us and always, if we managed the crossing in less than ten minutes, he complimented us. If by any chance he did not go on an expedition with us, Carl usually occupied the back seat, brass watch in hand, varying the usual timing game by counting aloud the strokes we took, one of us in each rowing seat, praising us, as father did, if we cut the crossing to seven or eight minutes or if, by tremendous, long strokes, done with all the power of our arms and backs, we reduced the record of strokes by five or ten. Now and then Carl would join in the rowing and someone else would be given the honor of holding the precious brass watch.

If we went on berry hunts we did so in a fierce spirit of competition to see who could first fill his bowl or tin. By these and other means nearly every job we did turned into a game or race, usually with Carl as the judge. As we grew older we began to understand that, whatever the job, he was the natural organizer and manager.

A distant cousin, Lodvar Boe, arrived one summer from Norway and quickly was taken into the family and introduced to our little customs. He was big and sturdy and plunged into our work and play with great spirit. He learned our signs and whistles readily, including "two fingers," which meant "Let's go swimming." And he had much to teach us about swimming. He was a long-distance swimmer of prodigious strength, as we thought, and he won a reputation one day by taking a long bamboo pole out with him on a swim, trolling down along the shore, and actually catching a fish of some size. That had never been done before. He was much older than I and had no difficulty in carrying me on his back for long swims.

The boys of the family were curious about an old, battered Norwegian chest that Lodvar owned, and we pined to get into it and explore its contents. Particularly we wanted to know how much money Lodvar had. But he kept the chest a locked mystery to us and never would divulge his riches, with the result that we built up in our minds pictures of fabulous wealth concealed in the chest. Lodvar came and after a summer went, the chest with him, and we were none the wiser. He himself departed for the Dakota prairies, where, many years later, some of us visited him and found him a prosperous farmer.

Since Lodvar was older than we were, our parents entrusted him with some responsibility for looking after us, seeing that we kept out of mischief and behaved ourselves. We played tricks on him, which in general he took with good nature, for he had a sense of humor, but occasionally he was annoyed by our pranks and tried to catch us, invariably trying to beguile us with the magic sign of "two fingers." We knew his game, however, and eluded him if we could.

One day while we were swimming, not at the old tree but alongside our own dock, a snake swam out from under the boat slide onto the water. There was a mad and excited dash by all of us to get out of its way, then an equally exciting chase to catch and kill it, each one of us armed with any stick that we were able to snatch up. We caught the snake and to our astonishment discovered that it was not the usual grass snake or brown snake, but, as we thought, a rattlesnake, the one and only instance in all our Minnetonka summers of our seeing a poisonous snake. We were proud

and fascinated, and Lodvar and my oldest brother, Hal
(who later became a doctor), dissected the poisonous glands
of the rattler while the other boys stood in a ring around
the surgeons, everyone watching with intense interest, but
keeping a discreet distance, for one could never tell when a
dead snake might suddenly come alive. After careful ma-
neuvering Lodvar and Hal extracted what they believed to
be the poison glands, and we all marched in triumph to tell
mother and father of our exploit. They were at first incred-
ulous, but when father saw the snake he agreed that it was
a rattler, to our satisfaction. If he had any doubts, he did
not betray them. For some days at the lake front we were
wary. If one rattlesnake, why not more? But we never saw
another.

Lodvar also taught us to trap and skin animals, and we
exhibited the hides on the walls of the carpenter's shop built
just behind the shower house, always leaving room for the
salted heads of large pickerels. We also experimented with
a menagerie, principally for squirrels and chipmunks, using
cracker boxes that we fitted up with screens.

The outdoor playground in summer naturally posed
some small problems for us in adjusting our life when we
returned to city life in the autumn, but fortunately we had
an immense attic in our Minneapolis house after we moved
away from the Augsburg campus. This became a playground for us, and our use of it sometimes had untoward
results. We fitted up, for example, an air-rifle range and
invited our playmates in to match their skill with ours.
There was a small problem of a suitable target, but this was
solved by John, when he found what appeared to be an old
and discarded hat box that was ideally suited for our marks-
manship. We set it up at one end of the attic against a wall
that could absorb our shots without damage to the house,

and then proceeded to puncture the box with many shots —
not too difficult a target.

At the climax of one of our shooting sessions father
stalked up the attic stairs to survey the scene. When he saw
the target he was horrified and instantly stopped our game.
He rushed to the box, opened it, and took out of it his one
and only high silk hat! The glossy top hat, carefully put
away for a dress occasion, had scores of perforations! I do
not recall any profanity — he was not given to its use
though a crisis of major proportions might provoke certain
curious expletives that we considered definitely profane in
spirit. But we all remember the dismay with which he
looked at the utter ruin of his noble headpiece.

We were one of the first families in our Minneapolis
neighborhood to acquire a punching bag, and this we also
installed in the attic. We rightly regarded a session at the
bag as a privilege for anybody, and so we charged a penny
for a stated number of minutes in the game of punching —
a practice that we were not able to keep up beyond the
initial period of novelty. The attic was also the scene of
action after Carl won a magic lantern as a prize for a school
composition published in the *Minneapolis Journal Junior*.
The lantern, with its oil-burning light, was a neighborhood
sensation, and we arranged a show, charging the usual
admission of one cent. The slides were of the Holy Land
and the story of Robinson Crusoe. The proceeds from one
performance, as recalled by some members of the family,
were sixteen cents.

Games and family life alike had their rules. Father himself did not smoke, and smoking was forbidden in the
household though not, of course, by guests. We had no difficulty in finding ways of evading the rules father and mother
laid out, however. We gathered up ripe, blackened sweet

clover, crumbled it in our hands, fashioned cigarettes from any kind of paper available, and smoked them, feeling daring and smart. And dried corn silk was, we thought, an almost perfect tobacco.

We also collected the stems of water lilies, laid them out to dry, and, when they were brown and brittle, lighted these enormously long cigarettes. When absolutely nothing else was available, we might use string, curled up and wrapped in a convenient paper. If its taste left something to be desired, especially as compared with that of clover or lily stems, it was, after all, a cigarette of a kind. Then we discovered kinnikinnick, the famed Indian tobacco. After we had learned to identify it, we gathered up its leaves, dried them, rolled them in our hands, and stuffed the particles into acorn pipes or improvised cigarette papers. We also used the dried clover in our pipes.

The time came when we experimented with tobacco. I had put aside a little capital from some frog deals when I ventured to buy a package of Duke's Mixture. I got a sheaf of cigarette papers with the tobacco, and rolled my first real cigarette. I managed to survive the experience without a sign of sickness, but the problem of hiding the Duke's Mixture so that it would not be seen by father and mother was serious. I slipped it under the front porch and protected it, as I thought, by a large stone. Alas, it was not sufficiently protected, for when I next hunted it out some animal, perhaps a squirrel, had torn the package open and scattered about or eaten the tobacco.

After smoking real tobacco, the central problem was to disguise the smell so that father and mother could not find us out. I used to go to the garden, dig up vegetables, especially onions, and eat with the hope of smothering the telltale tobacco odor by a stronger but wholly respectable one.

On one occasion in town, I had been sent off on an errand by my mother — an errand that I performed somewhat grudgingly because it came at dinner time. As a gesture of defiance in absentia, for nobody went with me, I lighted a cigar and smoked part of it on the way home. Unfortunately for me, I arrived just as father, who always conducted devotions at the end of the dinner (or supper, as we called it), was beginning the closing prayer. I slipped into my chair next to mother. Father was praying, heads were bowed, hands folded, and mundane thoughts were supposedly banished for a few minutes. But mother, unfortunately, had an acute sense of smell. This I knew, and I was uncomfortable as I sat beside her, for she would not miss the strong, and to her offensive, smell of the cigar. In the middle of the prayer, I noted out of the corner of my eye that she turned her head slightly. An instant later I thought I heard her sniff faintly, and a few instants later, though I meanwhile protected myself by bending even lower over my plate and edging slightly away from her, I caught another turning movement. Father went on with the prayer, a long one that I devoutly hoped would last for an hour or two. But it came to its ending Amen. Everybody left the table, including mother, but I knew that a conference was inevitable. I ate as fast as I could, snatching up all items of food that might counteract the smell of tobacco. All to no avail. As I was nearing the end of my supper, mother returned, sat down next to me, asked about my errand, and worked up to the question I was expecting: "Theodore, have you been smoking?"

Statesmanship did not indicate a lie, though I had weighed the practicability of one. "Well," I said, "I did take a few puffs." Mother said, "A few puffs of what?" I said, "Oh, something I lighted." She said, "What did you light?"

I speculated on the likelihood that she would accept a story of something other than tobacco, but an inner voice told me that this would scarcely explain away the smell, and so I said, "Well, I had a little cigar." This was definitely stretching the truth, for the cigar was wholly standard in size and shape. Mother had an appalling instinct for the right question. "How little?" she asked. I put out my two forefingers in a feeble and inexact gesture, but she asked me to measure the length precisely. There was no escaping her logic, and so I told the full truth. She did not discipline me, but talked about the evils of smoking and told me how sad it made her that I should be falling a victim to the pernicious habit. I was ashamed and meek and did not smoke a cigar again — for some time.

Father was a story teller who knew many folk tales, some of which in a later day we read in the collections of Asbjörnson and Moe and Hans Christian Andersen, but the stories that made the deepest impression were a few out of his own home background, some of them tinged with superstition. In our lake house we had a narrow stairway running up to the second floor, and sometimes father would make vague allusions to the staircase in his old house in Norway. We asked him questions, but he would edge away from our direct questions and shake his head as if the truth were a little too much for us to stand. What we wormed out of him, however, was that in his ancient house there was a staircase that had secrets and strange powers. He hinted that on certain occasions when boys had been disobedient or had lied, they might find it dangerous to walk up that staircase. As they went up, the walls of the stairs had a way of narrowing, until, halfway up, they would catch young sinners and squeeze them to death. Had this actually happened, we would ask. Could he tell us more?

Who was squeezed to death? Could he name somebody? Had he seen it happen? How could a staircase get narrower as one walked up it? What made it close in? But when we put such questions to father, he would look at us gravely and intimate that he could not tell us more. He would then glance at our own staircase. No, he had better not tell us more! And we walked up the stairs wondering if some dark power might not close in on us, hold us tight, and squeeze the life out of us!

Father liked riddles and enjoyed testing our wits with them. According to my brother John, he kept a book of riddles from which he drew questions to ask us, but this I do not recall. I remember, however, that he would ask us to tell him what tree grows with its roots up and its top down, and what it is that goes all day long but doesn't move from the spot — these and many others.

A student of child behavior has written that in the thirty years after 1900 "the proportion of children carrying on self-initiated and participant activities, such as making collections and developing other hobbies, decreased enormously in various levels, while the proportions in spectator, listening, or viewing activities increased by a corresponding amount." I do not know just how evidence has been gathered for this generalization, but I do know that in our childhood, both at Minnetonka and in town, we engaged unendingly in hobbies.

We were all stamp collectors, and we watched father's mail vigilantly, for his correspondence reached out to India, Madagascar, Norway, Russia, and other countries, and there was always rivalry to capture the exotic stamps that had carried the missives on their long way. Customarily he returned letters to their envelopes after he had read and answered them, and in his desk and on his shelves were large packets, usually held together with binders or string. As one thumbed through these packets, it was unusual to find a letter that had not had its stamps cut off. Not infrequently he received packages of reports or books, their wrappers bright with stamps, and when that happened there was a scramble to establish priority of claim to the treasures.

On the theory that we were learning a little geography and history, father himself took a friendly interest in our collecting, though he was not himself a collector, and from time to time he would furnish us with the names of correspondents in far countries who might be interested in trading with us. So we wrote to his friends, offering to send handsome collections of United States stamps in exchange for the stamps of Madagascar, India, and other places. I recall a correspondence with someone, perhaps a consul, in Tahiti that added choice items to our collections. Ultimately we built large and valuable collections, particularly of Norwegian, Madagascar, and India stamps.

My brother John and I, in our later boyhood, started a stamp company of our own — "The Gopher Stamp Company" — with our Minneapolis address as headquarters. Using an attic room as our office, we set up sheets of stamps with the catalogue price and our own much reduced sale price indicated below each item, advertised, offered agents discounts of fifty percent on sales, and mailed stamps out to a fairly wide clientele. Naturally we featured the countries for which we had the greatest number of duplicates. The company flourished for some time, but people had an exasperating way of failing to return our sheets or to send us the money they owed us, and ultimately the Gopher Stamp Company went bankrupt and ceased to exist. While it lasted we put every penny we earned — from odd jobs and carrying newspapers — into it.

Throughout our boyhood we bought catalogues, secured the best stamp books we could find, studied geography, learned the names of countries and of their kings, and informed ourselves about the stamps they had issued. As the years went by our collections were mainly consolidated in the hands of John, though Hal as a doctor resumed the hobby and became the owner of a very good and valuable United States collection. During the forty or more years that Carl has lived in Greece he has regularly sent John copies, used and unused, of the issues of that country, and as a result John has a splendid Greek collection.

Naturally, the stamp hobby was more an indoor, city diversion than a Minnetonka activity, but father's mail continued to come in through all the months of the year, and we did not ordinarily permit any foreign stamps of his summer mail to go uncollected. We traded stamps in a wide circle of collectors, always with an eye to our advantage in any bargains we struck, and I am afraid that when we fell in with someone innocent of stamp values, we managed to separate him from his stamps at very low prices and at the same time to convince him of the extraordinary value of the stamps we offered for sale or barter.

Stamps represented only one of many forms of collecting in which we were interested. Carl made a hobby of railroad timetables and, year after year, tried to get a copy of every timetable available at the stations in Minneapolis. He would pore over train schedules, learn them by heart, and astonish the family by the precision of his information as to when what train left Minneapolis for where, by what railroads and transfers one got from Minneapolis to New Orleans, New York, or San Francisco. He was even prepared, at a moment's notice, to plan the transportation details of a trip to Europe. We also collected shells, carnelians, birds' eggs,

marbles, "election cards," in later days butterflies and insects, and indeed just about everything to which any value
could be attached — particularly trading value.

We also took note of certain elevations that looked to us
suspiciously like Indian mounds. These we found in the
woods bordering the lake, and we had visions of treasures
to be unearthed. So on several occasions we set out — a
little furtively because we were not certain that our parents
would approve of grave digging — with spades and hoes to
excavate our mounds. Unhappily we turned up nothing but
the roots of near-by trees, and we failed to add Indian relics
to our collections. Fortunately for the archaeologists of a
later day, we did not include in our researches any of the
genuine Indian mounds in the vicinity of "Mound" — a
place we occasionally visited.

We did not do much reading in the summertime, but
during the months in town we made intensive use of home
books (including a many-volume American encyclopedia)
and of the branch library not many blocks away from our
house. Without much guidance we read everything we
could lay our hands on and reread many times such favorites as *Tom Sawyer, Huckleberry Finn*, and *Cudjo's Cave*.
Father was concerned about our reading, and from time to
time he would inquire about, and even explore, the books
we carried home. He felt that my own reading was degenerating when, in a heavy splurge of G. A. Henty, I was
absorbed in reading a novel entitled *The Treasure of the
Incas*. It was a fairly good historical novel, but it had a lurid
cover, and father, perhaps not wholly ignorant of the fact
that we smuggled nickel and dime novels into the house
(and hid them in the attic or under our mattresses), decided
to give the Henty book a critical inspection. He confiscated
it, to my dismay, and proceeded to read it. It seemed to the

family that he read it with an interest definitely greater than that of a disinterested judge concerned about the quality of books selected by his children. At any rate, he finished the reading to the last page, and thereafter, for some weeks, placed some limitations upon my choice of books, an action that I naturally resented.

Events and persons stand out most vividly in one's memory of past times, but this story would be incomplete if it did not recall sounds and smells and sights which, though not peculiar to Minnetonka, seemed a part of its seasoning and flavor.

There were melancholy sounds — the wailing of loons in flight across the lake, and the plaintive call of the wild dove, interpreted by us as meaning, "More rain, more rest." The chorus of frogs croaked to us evening after evening. When the sun was hot, one heard the whir of the cicadas, which we called "locusts." Spring was not spring without the hail of the meadowlark, and a summer day lacked character without the caw of the crow. Night after night one was lulled to sleep by rhythmic palpitations from the edge of the lake that seemed as endless as time itself. And there was a mystery about sounds at night — the faint barking of dogs, the far-away whistle of a train, the distant rumble of thunder, now and then the weird and explosive screech of an owl.

There was always the sound of water in its changing moods, the lazy wash of waves when winds were light, the plops of fishes leaping out of water at night — sounds that carried far when nature was still. When rains came sweeping across the lake, one heard first a distant patter, then a crescendo of sound as billions of drops struck the lake surface in a wild advance usually accompanied by the crash of thunder.

The sound of rain on the roof was even more familiar to us than that of rain on the lake, for home was sanctuary in storm — and often the rains came at night or in early morning. Every summer we heard the patter of drizzles, the hard beating of steady downpours, and the fury of violent rains driven by gusts of wind that shook the house while we snuggled under blankets. We knew also the staccato drumming of hail, which caused us to rush out of the house to gather up pieces of ice, each of us trying to find the biggest.

After a day and night of clouds and rain, we often had clear skies, with the wind blowing out of the northwest, and then air and earth, with their freshness and purity, filled us with a sense of well being and the joy of living.

Not less characteristic than sounds were the smells of Minnetonka life — that of burning leaves and brush in spring, and of hay and clover freshly cut in summer, the fragrance of flowers in the garden or along the roadside and in the woods, the odors of decaying fish along the lake shore, the evil smell of scum on swamps and lake in late summer, and the penetrating, if sometimes faint, emanations of that perennial but furtive visitor, the lowly, striped skunk.

The sights were those familiar to all lakeland — sunsets of glory, with changing colors in the glowing sky; the silver track of the moon shining across the rippling lake surface; the dark silhouette of the opposite shore as details faded into mass; the flash of tanagers and orioles flying from tree to tree; the darting grace of the hummingbird; the quiet dignity of a blue heron poised at some lonely spot in the rushes; the antics of squirming pollywogs in near-by creeks and swamps; rainbows that circled the sky; and nights of stars that made one wonder whether the universe had any end, and where Heaven's gates were.

Familiar things, these sights and smells and sounds, all about us through the long summers, and taken for granted, with little speculation about meanings in nature and life. As time dissolved the precision of memory, the impressions merged into a composite, smells mingling with sounds and both with scenes, the whole helping to recall the setting of summer life.

IV

FISHING AND HAZARDS

FISHING was remarkably good in Lake Minnetonka. All summer long we caught sunfish, crappies, and black bass in abundance. Like all fishermen, we had favorite spots — "Sunken Island" in West Arm, the narrows between West Arm and Jenning's Bay, various places along Fagerness Point, North Arm, Stubb's and Maxwell's bays, the shore of bullrushes near Deering's Island, and Harrison's Bay. Often we made the long trip to that bay to catch pickerel. Time after time we pulled in pickerel of eight or ten pounds or more. Every large fish caught was weighed and exhibited, and if its size warranted more than ordinary pride, we nailed the head to the wall of the tool shed for visitors to admire. Carl and I, trolling in West Arm on one occasion, had a mighty strike. Carl, holding the line, announced that he had a big one. He called on me to row as fast as I could and gradually to make for shore. At last, with the fish still on, we came alongside the old swimming tree. My brother handed the line to me and then jumped into the water. As I brought the big fellow up, Carl put his hand over the head, with his thumb and third finger in the eye sockets, and lifted in a fourteen-pound pickerel — a family record.

Though a record for us, the fourteen-pounder was not the prize catch of the shore. One day N. N. Ronning, a favorite to all in the community because of his wit and storytelling ability, came out to the lake, went fishing in the direction of Harrison's Bay and presently returned with an eighteen-pound Northern. When we heard the story of how he had caught it we were disgusted. It had struck in the channel between West Arm and Harrison's Bay and promptly got entangled in a huge mass of weeds. All Mr. Ronning had to do was to haul in a heavy weight, gather it up, and find at the center the largest pickerel caught in those waters in all the years we were there. "A city man," we said unfairly, "who knows nothing about fishing comes out, hooks a big one, and hauls it in without a fight. If the fish had struck in open water, he would have lost it, but tangled in weeds as it was, nobody could lose it." What we really meant was why didn't that pickerel strike on our line? What business did a city man (we ignored the fact that he once owned a cottage at the lake) have to come out and snatch that prize out of our hands? Before we were through with it, we almost imagined that we had had the fish on our lines and that Mr. Ronning had stolen it from us. A city man!

Father was a good fisherman. True enough, he almost always sat in the back seat when he went out with us. He held the line. We did the rowing. But he had a discerning eye for water, gave us explicit directions where to go, and handled a fish well. Unless he had a small pickerel, he invariably tired the fish by playing it, then brought it up and put his fingers in its eye sockets to lift it into the boat. He had little patience in his still-fishing. He gave the sunfish only a few moments — if they did not quickly begin to nibble, he would say, "Pull up the anchor, boys. We move." In the end he usually found the right spot.

On fishing expeditions he often told us tales of fishing as he knew the sport when a boy in Norway, of trips to mountain streams where, with his brothers, he caught brook trout. He had a belief in the effect of the moon on fishing, and when the new moon made its appearance, he would say, "Now we must go fishing. This is a fishing day!" Then there was a rush for bait — angleworms and grubworms, occasionally grasshoppers or clams, minnows, perch caught off the dock, and frogs, the latter carried in home-made, green-painted frog boxes. For snaring pickerel, father liked to use enormous spoonhooks adorned by himself with gaudy red-cloth wrappings. When boat and poles and lines were in order and all our preparations were completed, off we would go, each boy devoutly hoping that he would have the honor of catching the first fish.

Johnny was the luckiest of the boys. Father reports that when John was only five or six and used a fishing pole only as many feet long as he was years old, with a short line, he usually caught the first fish. When we fished sunfish with angleworms, it seemed that his hook had a special magic, and often he was the one who added excitement to the day's events by pulling in a big black bass. The love of fishing has remained with him through the years, and he is still the most devoted and indefatigable fisherman of the family.

We did not use rod and reel. When we went for bass, we always fished with what we called "bass poles" — very long bamboo poles, with frog as bait. Sometimes we fished without cork in deep water, often we fished along the shore, with corks only a few inches above the bait, and we learned how to drop our bait with precision at tiny openings in the lily pads, where the black bass lurked. In deep summer we knew certain places where the bass played in deep water, and our neighbors wondered how we could come in with large catches when they were getting none. The answer was simple. We rowed to Maxwell's Bay — a long row — found our spot, trailed our frogs twenty feet down in the water, and not infrequently caught our limit.

One of the tasks father assigned to us again and again was that of taking visitors out for large fish. We were the rowers and guides, and if any fish were caught we also were saddled with the job of cleaning them — an art in which we all became experts (at least in our own estimation). As we viewed these inexperienced urban fishermen, we formulated a philosophy about them. Unless they believed that they would catch fish, they would not catch fish. Again and again we took out somebody who lolled in the back seat, talked to us about people, religion, philosophy, and life, paid no attention to the line, regarded the lake with disfavor, was under the impression that the fish were ill-bred because they did not compliantly snap at the hook, wearied quickly, and asked us to row him ashore. Again and again we went out alone after such an experience, fished in the same spots, and caught one fish after another. "Unless you are interested and believe you are going to be lucky, you never will be lucky," we said. When we got somebody who had the will to catch fish, we were ready to row our arms and heads off for him — and usually he went in with a fine catch.

We had not read Izaak Walton in those days, but we should have agreed with *The Compleat Angler* that God never made a better recreation than angling. And we probably should have accepted also his theory that angling is "so like the mathematics that it can never be fully learnt." We caught innumerable black bass along the shores of Forest Lake at dusk. Once Carl played a vicious ten-pound Northern on pole and line from the prow of our boat in the reeds near Deering's Island, with John rowing the boat for some fifteen minutes, following the rushes of the fish as Carl tired him out. Sometimes we left in the morning from the home dock to be gone all day, with lunches packed by mother for the excursion, and usually we came home with long strings of bass and pickerel. We fished on every shore and in every kind of weather. Sometimes we waded out as far as we could in Crystal Bay, near the channel connecting it with North Arm, and hauled in bass after bass. Like all fishermen, we tended to go far from our home when we wanted to make glamorous catches. Distant waters seemed better, but often we had our best luck within talking distance of our own dock. On one occasion, pulling up what seemed to be a bass or pickerel, we landed a soft-shell turtle that dashed around our boat with terrifying agility and nearly caused all of us to dive into the lake to escape its menace. Father once caught an enormous dogfish in Cook's Bay that managed, despite his every precaution, to leap out of the boat after it was safely landed.

Some years ago I came upon a diary kept by a pioneer woman who traveled west in a covered wagon. In it she tells of Beauty, the pet dog of her caravan, who one day was crushed by one of the heavy wheels of a wagon. The emigrants stopped and buried Beauty with due ceremony, and everyone, young or old, felt sad. The story reminded me of "Ornis," our canary. When, one summer day, she died, there was sorrow in the family. Father superintended and Hal conducted the funeral, both of them with solemnity and dignity. We put "Ornis" in a box covered with pansies and buried her on a hillside near a favorite Whitney crab-apple tree.

One day a man with a gun stopped at our house. He was a hunter, he explained, and needed a cup of coffee to refresh his spirits. Mother gave him a cup of coffee, and then the boys followed him down the country road that ran behind our house. As soon as we were out of earshot from mother, the hunter let himself go. He was, he said, the damned best hunter in the world. He never missed a shot, blankety-blankety-blank — and he rolled off such a string of oaths as we never had heard before in our lives. Every sentence that came from his mouth was punctuated by fine and unusual swearing, and we listened with admiration to the splendid flow of words that, if we knew them, were forbidden in our circles, or if we did not know them were of such a resounding, ear-filling character that we instantly committed them to memory for possible future use.

In the midst of a roaring sentence filled with oaths of the most blood-curdling kind, the hunter spied a squirrel some rods ahead, motioned us all to be quiet, raised his gun, took aim, and fired.

The shot caught the squirrel in the head. It squirmed, turned over, and was motionless.

"Boys," shouted the hunter, "bury the blank, blank, blank, blankety-blank little cuss. Pick up that dirty little, blank, blank, blankety-blank beast and bury him."

"Why not just throw him into the woods?" one of the boys asked.

"No, Sir, no, sirree!" said the hunter. "Bury him. Bury the low-lived, son-of-a-blank, blank, blankety-blank, blank beast. Bury him. It's against my religious principles, boys, not to give a decent burial to that blank, blank, blankety-blank of a beast."

We went home after burying the squirrel, and father casually asked us what kind of man the hunter was.

"Oh," we said, "he had religious principles."

A stranger on a Sunday morning took one of the boats along the shore — by what authority we never knew — erected a mast in it, and then proceeded to ballast the boat with what we boys thought was a dangerous load of large rocks picked up near the beach. A strong wind was blowing, and we ventured, timidly, to suggest that he had better not go out in the blustery morning, with squalls sweeping across the lake, and with so small a boat fitted with so large a sail, plus the hazard of the many big rocks. But he waved our comments aside and started out.

We saw him sailing at a fine pace straight out across West Arm and then, making a half turn, toward Spring Park. It looked as if he knew his business, and so we turned to other matters, but some of us kept an eye on him. Suddenly, when he was veering over toward Fagerness Point, his boat went over. It was quite too far for us to do anything about it, and so we simply stood and watched. Either the man could not swim or else he was too stupid about the hazards of the lake to cling to the boat. At any rate he bobbed about in the water for a few seconds — we could scarcely make him out in the distance — and then he disappeared. We saw only the boat, overturned, its mast down in the water, with no sign of the sailor.

Of course we rushed up to the house to tell father about the tragedy, but it was too late to do anything about it. Another drowning at Minnetonka! Who he was we never knew. We only remembered him as a foolish man who would not take advice from youngsters. We knew better, but he paid for his folly with his life.

One day when I was a boy I strolled down to the dock at our water front, walked out on it, looking at the water as I walked, and suddenly saw my sister Anne lying on the bottom of the lake alongside the dock, face up, absolutely still. How long she had been there I never found out, but of course I jumped in, lifted her out, rushed up to the shore with her, put her down, and presumably pummeled her and did everything an excited boy would do to try to restore her breathing while yelling as loudly as possible for help. She came to with surprising quickness, and the explanation doubtless was that she had fallen in just before I arrived at the dock. That is all I remember about this episode, but in later years I used to shudder at the thought that chance might have sent me off on a frog-hunting expedition at that particular moment, and she might have lain at the lake bottom alongside the dock for a half hour or more before anybody noticed her absence.

A drowning is stamped on my memory, and for a good reason: it resulted in the great run of my life, and of John's, too. A boy fell into the water from a near-by dock and was not pulled out until some minutes later. He was still and cold, and there was no sign of breathing. I do not remember what happened in the first minutes after he was found, but I do recall that John and I were chosen to go for a doctor. No cars, horses, or bicycles were available. Our job was to run for a doctor — and the nearest one lived on Crystal Bay, nearly two miles distant.

So Johnny and I, barefooted, excited, and proud of having been selected, started on a nonstop run. We did not set off at a mad pace. We decided to trot along as steadily as we could, knowing that if we ran too fast at the start, we should tire and probably would not make our destination in time.

Johnny was strong, tough, and two years older than I, but I was long-legged and fairly tough, too. We loped along, with never a stop, and checked every landmark along the way, saving our fastest running until we got within striking distance of the doctor's house. What our time was I do not know, but I remember that run as the most grueling run of my boyhood. We got there, found the doctor, gasped out our errand to him, and he promptly hitched a horse to a sulky and started back, while we trudged home. The boy was dead when the doctor arrived. Our run had been fruitless — but it became part of the saga of Saga Hill.

Another run, this one from our Forest Lake home, is not less vivid in my memory, but this was by myself. It happened many years after the dock episode. Anne was ill, and father and mother were worried. Something was wrong, and after the usual home remedies had been tried it was evident that this was more than a passing ache, perhaps dangerous. Father and mother were nervous and alarmed as the hours passed by and Anne got worse, not better. Finally in the evening they suddenly said that somebody must start for Minneapolis, get an automobile, come back to the lake, and take Anne in to a Minneapolis hospital in the morning.

This was about eight-thirty in the evening. There was a train into town at nine, but no passenger boat was available, or if there was one, it was too late to catch it. So I was asked to run for the train and catch it at Langdon Park, now Navarre.

I ran down the dark road, remembered the run Johnny and I had made many years earlier, and regulated my pace. Somehow I made it. A fast run without a stop for what seemed to me like two or three miles but is probably only a mile and a half. Made it, but just in the nick of time, for when I reached Langdon the train was there. I closed with a dash and jumped on a moving train. So I got into Minneapolis that evening, found a friend of the family who owned an automobile, and asked him to drive out to Minnetonka to get my sister. We reached our lake house before breakfast time the next morning and got Anne to Minneapolis. A doctor diagnosed her trouble as acute appendicitis, but for some reason (probably a good reason in that pre-penicillin day) he delayed an operation for a day or two. When he did operate, the appendix had burst, and it was touch and go whether she would come through — but she did.

Let no one think that Minnetonka was only fair skies, friendly waters, and serene landscapes. It could be storm — furious, with winds beating upon the houses, lightning flashing, thunder exploding, rain hurtling down in torrents. Once father and I, returning from Spring Park in our rowboat, were caught in a storm of lashing fury. Luckily we had two pairs of oars. Father, realizing that a near-tornado was upon us, began to row in quick strokes, shouting to me to keep in time with him, and we made for the nearest shore, the tip of Fagerness (the "beautiful point"). Nearly every wave broke water into the boat, and before we got to shore, the water in the boat was well above our ankles. When we managed to get into shallow water, we jumped out of the boat and hauled it onto shore, then made our way home by a long, roundabout walk to find mother waiting for us, anxious, but, as usual, calm.

Another time a tornado skipped our house but struck the "beautiful point" with screaming fury and destroyed many of its houses. While the storm was mounting, Carl, John, and I sat at the lake shore watching trees snap off across the lake, west of Deering's Island, and admiring the mountainous waves lashed up by the wind. In the midst of the tumult mother, frightened, came down to the shore. "Boys," she called, "don't you know there's a great storm? Come to the house at once!" We ran up the path and when, half way up, a tree some rods away toppled over, we doubled our speed. The day after this storm we all walked to the point to see the damage and wonder at the terrible power of the wind.

We learned the ways of the lake, watched the signs of weather, and normally sought shore, wherever we might be, when clouds and thunder warned us of danger. I remember tense moments when Johnny and I cowered under the bridge between West Arm and Crystal Bay while the skies seemed to be falling.

Sometimes moments of danger were preceded not by the rumble of thunder but by ordinary amenities, as for instance the affair in which father became a hero. A neighbor from up the shore, Mrs. Moe, with her daughter Ragnhild, rowed two visiting ladies to our place for afternoon coffee. As they landed at the dock, Mrs. Moe, a very petite person, got out first. The two ladies, one of them not precisely petite, then started to get out, both at the same time, and of course the boat tipped over and they landed in the water. They grasped the edge of the dock with their hands, kicked their legs, and screamed. The water was fairly shallow, and they could easily have waded ashore, but they thought they were in imminent danger of drowning. Father, meanwhile, aware of the approaching landing, had started down hill to greet the visitors with his usual courtesy. The moment he realized that a tragedy was impending, he rushed at top speed for the dock, valiantly lifted one of the victims out of the water, and guided the other, somewhat too substantial for him to lift up, to shore and safety. Dripping, and their long skirts swishing, the ladies were escorted up the long hill. Mother rushed them to a bedroom, got off their wet clothes, dressed them in dry clothes (with some slight difficulty in the case of the buxom lady), and then proceeded calmly with the coffee party.

That night, after the children had gone to bed, we heard mother and father laughing, but mostly father.

Mother had a way of laughing quietly, her body shaking, tears running down her cheeks. The picture of father saving her two austere lady guests and hauling them ashore, wet to their underclothes, was too much for mother. She laughed then — and always afterward when she recalled the day father was a hero. But hero he was, to us and to our neighbors.

The wonder is that there were not more drownings than there were along our shores. As children we had no fear of the water. Notwithstanding instructions and cautions, we often "fell in," but we took such episodes as a matter of course, shed our clothes (normally a pair of overalls and a blue or black shirt), and dried them carefully before going home. We never reported such trifles to father and mother. It was difficult for us to understand the inability of town children to swim. On one occasion a cousin from St. Paul, Ed Olsen, spent a few days with us at the lake. He could not swim a stroke, and this was beyond our comprehension. So we took him out in our boat, some distance beyond his depth. Rightly reading and fearing our intentions, he jumped into the lake and, landing on the bottom, instinctively (and fortunately) headed for shore. Presently we saw the tips of his fingers appear above water, then the top of his head, finally his nose and mouth. He came clear, waded ashore, and took it all in good spirit, without resentment, though obviously we had endangered his life. Our treatment of Douglas, another cousin, was even less defensible. Far beyond his depth, we forced him to get out of the boat, hang onto the edge, then drop, kick his legs, and grab the boat again. Happily he survived this cruel form of pedagogy. It was Douglas, by the way, who, hearing about the "Deaconess Home," surprised us by asking "What does Mr. Deaconess do?" Douglas, his two sisters

Irene and Doris, and his younger brother Harold, children
of Aunt Clara and Uncle George, were all fun-loving, and
we rejoiced at Saga Hill when their family occupied a
near-by cottage.

V

CELEBRATIONS, TRIPS, AND NEIGHBORS

DROWNING or the fear of drowning did not much occupy
our minds, but we thought much about the Fourth of
July, both before and after that glamorous day. It is not
easy to recapture its magic as we knew it in the 1890's and
early 1900's. We looked forward to it, planned for it, and
put aside pennies and nickels earned from sales of frogs,
earnings from berry-picking, and odds and ends of money-
making. The climax was the evening fireworks, when
father, operating from a spot just below the coffee house, set
off skyrockets, roman candles, and red and green lights.
Along the shore families held similar celebrations, and the
evening was colorful, with some rivalry among the neighbors in the matter of height of skyrockets and magnificence
of display. One's cup of joy was full and running over
when father permitted each one of us to hold a roman
candle and swing it about in a grand circle as its stars shot
up into the darkness.

This was the official Fourth, the central event, but in
some respects the most exciting part of the day came earlier,
for every penny we had saved went into such specialties as
were in the market in those days, including firecrackers
that gave a long warning whistle before they exploded. We
bought, each of us, as many packages of firecrackers as our
budget permitted, and the day was punctuated by the
sharp explosions of our wares. Sometimes we shot off a
whole package at a time. Usually they went off singly, with
many a narrow escape from disaster as one or another of

us threw firecrackers up in the air, often at the last instant, without too much concern about the proximity of others.

Always there was rivalry in the matter of getting the largest possible firecrackers. One summer Carl suggested that we pool our resources and buy a cracker of such prodigious size that it would surpass anything ever known in the neighborhood. We joined him gladly in this adventure. Each of us chipped in to build up the treasury for the firecracker to end all firecrackers. The amount of money grew, and when Carl finally made the purchase, he got the largest firecracker we had ever seen, enormous, unheard of, a veritable cannon as it seemed to us.

We were cautious about handling it. It was something to see and admire, and no false modesty prevented us from showing it to the children of the hill. But we concealed it from our parents, for they might veto our firing off such a monster.

Unfortunately circumstances made it impossible for us to explode it on the Fourth of July. Carl was ill with meningitis, and it would be unfair to have our moment of glory without him. So we waited until he was well enough to join in the fun. After all, this was an event, not of a particular day, but of an entire summer. Naturally we wanted the right time, with everybody (except our parents) present. We craved an audience, and we were particular about choosing the right place. After careful study, we decided that the spot for the giant cracker was just behind a little structure (we ordinarily called it the "backhouse") that stood near the rear of our place, not far from the road. It would afford us a certain protection after we lighted the fuse, for we could rush down the yard, with that minor building between us and the bomb. And it was a fair distance from the house.

At last the fateful moment came. We all stood at a prudent distance. The great firecracker was put in place. Carl approached it with a match, struck it and lighted the long fuse, then ran toward us as if his life depended upon his speed.

A fateful instant of waiting, and then — there was a feeble spluttering, a wisp of smoke, and silence. No glorious blast, no terrific explosion, nothing but silence. The great anticlimax of our Saga Hill adventures. We edged up to the firecracker, ready to make a wild dash if it showed any signs of life, but it was inert, dead. We were disappointed, frustrated. We had expected such a mighty detonation as would topple over the small building whose name was rarely mentioned in our polite society. We had to content ourselves with the thought that never in all the years at Saga Hill had anybody owned a bigger firecracker than the one we bought that summer. But the event scarcely invited boasting. We might have learned something from our experience, but I do not recall that we indulged in any philosophical reflections on the perils of great expectations. We dismissed our sorrow and went swimming or started a game of shinny.

Great events in America and the world took place with relatively little notice from the younger set through the busy summer months of Minnetonka years, but we were aware of the Spanish-American War. Its actuality was brought home to us when Justin Blichfeldt came back from it in his Army uniform. We knew very little of what had happened to him, but we looked at him with admiring and envious eyes. As schoolboys we had marched on Decoration Day from our public school to Layman's Cemetery in Minneapolis to do honor to soldiers of the Civil War, but here was Justin, alive and in glittering uniform, a

soldier come home from a new war. The Civil War was
in the murk of the past — the Spanish-American War was
immediate. Justin was a hero to us.

We were in Minneapolis when President McKinley
came to town to join in celebrating the exploits and the
return from the Philippines of the Thirteenth Minnesota
Regiment, and father took us to a spot on Park Avenue
to watch the President go by in his carriage. But happily,
and to our great joy, we saw the President before the
parade. We walked with father, crossing the railroad
tracks on our way, and just as we arrived at the tracks, the
President's special train came gliding by, and there, on
the rear platform, stood the figure of the handsome William
McKinley — the President of the United States. So we
all cheered him, father swung his hat, and we felt that the
event marked us off from the ordinary people who lined
Park Avenue by the thousands. After all, we had practically
met the President personally, for when we waved and
shouted to him at the railroad tracks, he acknowledged our
cheers with a courtly wave of his hand and a smile. We felt,
after that happening, that we knew President McKinley,
and when he was shot and died a year or two later we
grieved as for a friend.

Justin Blichfeldt's glory as a soldier paled when compared with the exploits of Hal. First of all, he was chosen
by father to accompany him on a trip to Norway in 1898
— Hal was then thirteen. In letters we heard echoes of
Hal's adventures. He crossed the ocean in a great ship of
the "White Star Line." He stood with father in a London
street, near Westminster Abbey, to watch, in what father
termed a "mighty silence," the funeral of a man named
Gladstone. He saw the British Museum, and then went on
to Hamburg and Copenhagen. In the Danish capital father

and Hal spent a day with the United States Minister to Denmark, who took them on a tour of the city and showed them, among other things, the sculptures of Thorvaldsen. Then they went on to Norway, saw its capital, and at last visited "Bleken," the old home overlooking a beautiful valley, from which father as a young man had set out for America in the 1860's. Here father's own father and mother — then in their eighties — greeted them. A few days later they made their way to the Bleken mountain saeter, where they fished brook trout.

Hal, as the eldest son, won the glamorous prize of a European trip, but Carl, next in chronological line, achieved a distinction the same summer which, in our eyes, was scarcely less to be envied. He blossomed out as the owner of a bicycle, the first in the family, and the summer witnessed his efforts to master the art of cycling, from which to this day he bears a scar!

A half dozen summers later Hal persuaded mother and father to let him take a job at the World's Fair in St. Louis. This job, to our minds, was comparable to that of President or ambassador. It was nothing less than that of a chairman — that is, a guide who pushed a chair around the grounds with a visitor comfortably seated in it. How much Hal earned that summer we never knew, but his many letters home, each envelope decorated with colored pictures of the "St. Looey Fair," as we all called it, were thrilling. And when one day a letter arrived telling us that he had had the honor of transporting Alice Roosevelt herself — the Princess Alice — we were consumed with admiration and envy. Why couldn't we go to St. Louis and have the thrilling experience of pushing Alice around in a wheel chair? Why was all this glory Hal's alone? Alas, we did not get to the World's Fair, but after all, Hal was our brother, and we felt that somehow we shared his glory. So if anybody bragged about his family, we managed, by way of rebuttal, to work in some reference to Hal. "Yes, he's in St. Looey, at the World's Fair. Guess the name of the passenger he had in his chair! Alice Roosevelt!" And of course we whistled "Meet Me in St. Looey, Looey, Meet Me at the Fair" as if the fair practically belonged to us. When Hal came back we besieged him with questions about his adventures.

After the Sverdrups moved to Forest Lake, only a few steps from our place on West Arm, Harald Sverdrup was my constant companion and best friend. "Fatty," we called him, not in an ironical sense, but because he really was roly-poly. Every day his parents would send him, about noontime, for drinking water from our well, and we used every wile to delay his return home. Our great triumph was a day when he arrived shortly after noon and we prevailed on him to forget about his pail and join us in a fishing expedition from which we did not return until evening, much to the discomfiture of his parents. With Harald we went swimming, berrying in the woods, and berrypicking at near-by farms, where we were paid a cent or two a box for strawberries and raspberries. We were better berrypickers than Harald, but he was the life of the party, gay and debonair, never caring very much whether he kept up with us or not. He would eat berries from morning until late afternoon, his appetite never seeming to wane, and usually we were four or five boxes ahead of him when the time came to collect our pay. But he never was envious. He always had a good time, was never-ending in the jokes he played, a good companion. It was Harald who told us about a boy from town who, after lightning had struck a near-by tree, hunted for the volts.

We particularly enjoyed picking berries for a farmer named Carlson, who lived a mile or two away from Forest Lake. We never called him "Carlson." He had a way of dropping his r's, and we were quick to imitate him. We always called him "Cahlson." He fed us well, a little colony of children from Saga Hill who trudged down the country road to his place and were thrilled to earn sometimes as much as twenty or thirty or even forty cents a day picking berries. Once each summer we entertained the Carlson family at dinner, and invariably they repaid the courtesy by inviting us to dinner, Mr. "Cahlson" calling for us in his two-seated surrey (doubtless with a fringe on the top).

One of our neighbors was an accomplished pianist and music teacher whose skill I did not fully appreciate until many years later when I heard him play the Grieg Piano Concerto. We knew him in moments of a somewhat less artistic kind. Everybody on the Hill was intrigued by one slight mishap that overtook him. He had come out from town in a brand-new suit, and that evening had an encounter with a skunk, ordinarily friendly animals for which we had, if not affection, at any rate respect. The next morning he buried the suit in a freshly dug grave. The wife of the pianist had a passion for cleanliness. To our amazement she frequently swept her lawn with a broom, making one think — though the thought did not come until later years — of Mrs. Partington sweeping back the Atlantic Ocean. The pianist and his wife were exuberant folk who occasionally indulged in spirited and loud-voiced arguments. We enjoyed these debates immensely, and when one was on, with the voices of the protagonists carrying well out on the lake, we took delight in anchoring our boat within easy earshot. On one occasion the pianist strode down to his dock, interrupting what we thought was a particularly good husband-wife controversy, and in a furious voice shouted: "Boys, go away from here! Go out to the middle of the lake and fish! Go somewhere, wherever you please, but don't fish in front of my dock." We meekly pulled anchor and departed, though I am sure we wanted to retort that one simply could not catch sunfish in the middle of the lake — and the fishing was as good as the entertainment in front of his dock. And his dock was interesting to us. Here we saw our first launch when Harry Pence glided up to it with a lake vessel that did not have a smokestack. And the owners of the dock were interesting. We did not much understand the skill of the maestro at the piano or why he quarreled so exuberantly, but we did know that he was no ordinary mortal — if only because he had a horse and phaeton.

Another musician, John Blichfeldt, lived in the cottage next to ours, and we often heard him play the piano. Sometimes, on summer evenings, he enthralled us with duets played with a flutist named Oscar Owre. John Blichfeldt was more than a good piano performer and teacher (incidentally I "took lessons" from him in town) — he was also an actor who played parts in a Minneapolis stock company. His brother Frank was neither a pianist nor an actor, but he was a man of original ideas. Once he undertook to shingle the roof of the Blichfeldt house by starting from the top down instead of from the bottom up.

In days when stores were far away, a certain amount of borrowing and lending went on from house to house, and we were sometimes the messengers from our house to the Blichfeldts'. My mother always gave us careful directions, not only as to the particular item we were to ask for, but also as to certain polite words with which to preface our request. Invariably she instructed me to open along this line: "My mother asked me to bring you her very warm greetings and to ask you if you would kindly lend us a little sugar."

Martha on one occasion was instructed by mother to go to the Blichfeldts' and ask for the return of a rake they had borrowed. Martha's Norwegian pronunciation may have been a trifle faulty and Mrs. Blichfeldt was slightly deaf — at any rate, she interpreted Martha's words to mean that mother was inviting her to an afternoon party. "Thank you very much," said Mrs. Blichfeldt. "I shall be happy to come." At this point John interrupted, "It's not a party, Ma. Martha wants the rake!"

The Dahls and Moes lived at the farther end of Saga Hill, near a narrow channel (of great interest to us for its fishing) that ran between West Arm and Forest Lake. Borghild Dahl, nearly blind, liked to play croquet with us, but had difficulty in seeing the arches. Now and then we marked them with white handkerchiefs, but more frequently one of us would stand near the arch for which she was shooting. All her life she has fought blindness with courage, and she has told her story in an autobiography entitled *I Wanted to See.* "It was at our summer home at Lake Minnetonka," she writes, "that I had most of my fun during my childhood." She tells of playing out of doors "from early in the spring until late in the fall." Many years later, after she had become known as a writer, she wrote me that I was one of the boys who marked arches for her, and she had never forgotten that act. A memorable experience of my life, and I think also in hers, was an occasion when I introduced her as a novelist and biographer and she gave a speech to an audience on the campus of the University of Minnesota.

In introducing her, I did not use the nickname we gave her in childhood days — "Bolla."

Professor Wilhelm Pettersen was a poet and orator, and he looked like a sea captain — in fact he was the son of a sea captain. His own son, Egil, was one of my best friends, a playmate in town, but unaccustomed to lake life. It was almost incredible to us that he could not swim. Everybody in our circle could swim. Nobody learned to swim — we had always known how. We could not remember a time when we had not known how. And so, when Egil and his father came out to the lake and we all went swimming, it seemed strange to us to see Egil on the dock, cautious of touching the water, afraid to jump in, hopping back like a frightened deer when we splashed him. Presently his father, dressed immaculately, strolled down to enjoy the spectacle of happy children at play. Egil, unhappy, disconsolate, afraid, was on the dock — all the rest of us were in the water.

"Egil," said his father, "why aren't you in the water?"

"I don't believe I care to go in just now," he said.

"And why not?" thundered the bearded father.

"Well," the boy stammered, "I'm not quite ready. I'll go in in a little while."

"Egil," roared his father, "I believe you are afraid!"

Suddenly Professor Pettersen marched out on the dock, swept Egil up in his arms, strode to the very end of the dock and threw the boy in.

A splash, and down went Egil. He couldn't swim, and the water was beyond his depth. We were too stunned to make a move to help him, and as a matter of fact we couldn't grasp the fact that Egil was unable to swim. So we watched. Egil bobbed up and went down again, sputtering, making feeble motions.

Then Professor Pettersen, magnificent, with dignity,

never stopping to take off his long morning coat, jumped, got the boy, hauled him out, took him ashore, saw that he was all right, and stalked off, dripping but majestic.

Minnetonka was excitement and adventure, swimming and fishing, games and play, sights and sounds, work and rest, mystery and silence — but it was not the only summer world we knew. Now and then mother would break away from the lake life, taking one or several of her children on a trip to St. Peter and the country, to the farm home of grandmother and grandfather in Nicollet County. And that was romance for those lucky enough to be chosen for the trip. The summer father and Hal went to Europe, mother took all the rest of the family to the country for a visit. Our pulses raced as we entered upon the preparations, the packing, the dressing in our best clothes, the good-bys, the crossing of the lake in the boat to board the train for town, the excitement of the train ride and the transfer in Minneapolis to the Omaha Road for the long trip to St. Peter, nearly seventy-five miles away. Then the meeting of uncles and aunts, the drive in a surrey to grandmother's, and finally the old farm home — grandfather sitting on the porch puffing at his long meerschaum pipe with its silver top and red tassels (I have it in my library now), grandmother, with her Viking face, her kindly ways, her friendly interest in every grandchild. The farm itself was a fairyland, with its barn that opened a new world of games to us, its cows and pigs and horses, its wagons and buggies and machinery, the apple orchard, the country roads and fields, the growing crops, and the many uncles and aunts and cousins roundabout. Days became weeks, and presently it was time to go back, to dress once more in our Sunday best, and say good-bys to a world whose magic matched that of the lake. Even the annual steamboat trip on the "City of St. Louis" paled in its attraction when compared with a visit to the country, and when we were once more at Saga Hill, back to swimming and fishing and berry hunting, we never tired of telling about the wonders of the farm, the sights we had seen, and even our mishaps, such as Carl's jumping on a spike that nearly went through his foot. Visiting Nicollet County was like seeing Paris or Rome.

But it was good to get back to the lake and the woods again. There was a fascination about the woods that stretched behind our Minnetonka house and down along the lake toward Sandy Bay (we simply called it "The Bay"). We never tired of expeditions, now hunting for plants and flowers, often for black raspberries and blackberries, and now and then with air rifles for any kind of game we might spy. It happened sometimes, when three or four of us were deep in the woods, that we went each our own way and quickly lost sight of the others. The woods were lonely, and one could get lost in them. To guard against this hazard we adopted a whistling call, a melancholy triplet of sounds that carried a long way (the theme an imitation of the song of the redwinged blackbird). One always answered it, then the call was repeated and repeated again, while each person moved in the direction of the answering sound. I catch the theme of our whistle now and again in a symphony, and at once I am back again in the woods of Minnetonka.

ENVOI

IN 1952 my father wrote, and distributed in mimeographed form, the story* of his boyhood days at Lake Minnetonka in the 1890's and early 1900's.

In 1969 he decided that the Minnetonka story might be of interest to persons outside the family circle.

On the last day of his life my father finished this last book — a project he tackled with the same delight and zest he had when he started to write and publish as a young man, giving meticulous attention to every word, every comma, every semicolon. He made his last marginal note, and with my mother drove to the neighborhood post office to mail the manuscript to his publisher.

For Theodore Blegen this was the last chapter.

—Margaret Blegen Crum

---

*An augmented version of an address given September 13, 1947, at the Minnetonka Country Club at the luncheon session of the Minnesota Historical Society's twenty-first summer tour, printed in *Minnesota History*, 29:4, 289-99 (Dec. 1948).

The Blegen family in front of house at Saga Hill. From left to right, front row: Martha C. Blegen, Theodore C. Blegen, John Blegen. Back row: Lars O. Skrefsrud, John H. Blegen, Mrs. John Blegen, an unidentified boy.